MW00333603

STILL SMILING

How to Overcome Tragedy & Thrive!

Denise Chandler

STILL SMILING: HOW TO OVERCOME TRAGEDY & THRIVE!
Copyright © 2023 by Denise Chandler
ISBN 978-1-7362277-9-4 (Hard Cover)

Designed and Published by King's Daughter Publishing
Indian Trail, North Carolina 28079
www.KingsDaughterPublishing.com

Printed in the United States of America.

Table of Contents

Dedication

In loving memory of my dad, Denver Lee,
and my husband, Richard Chandler.

My heavenly heroes.

Introduction

Writing this book has been a tremendous challenge for me. First, I wanted to write from the heart. I did. I know some people may read this and be offended by the content—please know I am not trying to offend anyone. I am simply sharing my twisting, turning life story. Part of it, anyway. This book is my testimony. It offers a glimpse into how I have overcome the obstacles life has tossed my way. I want it to be a blessing to others, helping them to see that no matter how dark the tunnel, light is always on the other side. My hope is that this book encourages someone to not give up, to not leave their family, to not throw in that bloodied towel. If I can help just one person, that's enough. Due to the sensitive nature of some content, I have changed certain names to protect people's identities.

I understand first-hand what it's like to go through darkness and feel like no one is on my side—as if everything and everyone is against me. I also know what it's like to feel surprised and grateful for those who reached out to me, pulled me up off my knees and hugged me. And I know what it's like to be in love and to have that special person root for your success.

This book offers no magical remedies. What it does offer is inspiration and hope. Only you can complete your journey, but you don't have to do it alone. There are people in your life who want to help you succeed. Sometimes they're right in front of you and sometimes you need to search for those people. As the Bible says, *"Faith without works is dead."* (James 2:17).

So keep the faith, but also put in *the work*.

Foreword

A Regular Saturday

SATURDAY, MARCH 28, 2020: IT WAS A REGULAR SATURDAY. My husband Richard and I and our son Kodie lounged on the couch, watching a movie. The rest of the kids were tucked away in their rooms.

Abruptly, Richard jumped up and rushed to our bedroom. I heard a whirring sound—the sound of his nebulizer. Richard was giving himself a breathing treatment, which was normal. He had asthma. Afterward, he hopped into the shower. Again. Normal. However, once he was out, he texted me from the bedroom: Baby, can you come here?

I left Kodie on the couch, engrossed in whatever movie we were watching. When I got to the bedroom, Richard was still wrapped in his brown bath towel.

"What's wrong?" I asked. *"Why are you texting me? Why didn't you just call for me to come to you?"*

As I stepped closer to him, I saw that he was sweating profusely. "Babe," he said, "there's something wrong. I cannot breathe." *"What do you mean you can't breathe? You are talking to me."*

"I can't breathe."

I started to panic. He looked gray. *"Richard,"* I said, *"I'm about to call 9-1-1."*

"No."

"Then I'm calling Shareece." I dialed my sister's number.

"Take him to Beaumont," Shareece said.

"Okay." I hung up the phone then turned to Richard. *"We're going to Beaumont."*

Richard struggled to get dressed.

"Do you want me to help you?"

"I got it."

When he finally got his shirt and jeans on, I walked him to the car. He panted the entire time—even when he was sitting down in the passenger's seat.

I sprinted back into the house and shouted, *"Amber! Amber!"* Our seventeen-year-old daughter came running downstairs. "What? What's wrong?" Confusion clouded her face. "Why are you screaming like that?"

I gave her the quick version, words rushing half-coherently out of my mouth, but she understood the gist. *"Watch your siblings while I take your dad to the hospital."*

"Okay, okay," Amber said, clearly worried.

I grabbed my purse.

"Babe, I'm okay," Richard told me as I drove him to the hospital. "Calm down."

I was driving as if I were auditioning for The Fast and the Furious franchise. *"Richard, you are not okay."*

"I'm okay."

Within thirty seconds, it all changed. Richard's eyes grew wide. Terrified. Tears streamed down his face and his entire body became erect. I hit him and screamed his name, but he didn't respond.

Panic closed in on me as my foot urged the car faster. I fumbled with my purse on the center console to find my cell phone. I called my sister. *"Something is wrong!"* I shouted.

"Well, what's wrong?"

"I don't know. He's not responding!"

"Get him to wherever you can get him."

To this day, I regret making the decision to take him to the nearest hospital, the epitome of a "wherever you can get him" facility.

By the time I pulled up to the ER entrance, Richard had snapped out of whatever he was in. "Baby, I can hear you now," he said. "I am so sorry."

"What?" I was angry because I was scared. *"What do you mean you can hear me now?"*

"I don't know," Richard said, "I could hear you, but I just couldn't respond to you."

I rushed into the hospital, demanding that they give my husband a wheelchair. The staff honored my request, but they said, "You can't come in here." In other words, I had to leave my husband in a wheelchair at what I personally considered one of the worst hospitals in Detroit.

I had no choice; I complied.

Chapter One

The Last Christmas

I ALWAYS THOUGHT MY PARENTS WERE RICH. They weren't. But I always thought they were because at Christmas, my siblings and I would each have our own gift section, which usually was huge. One Christmas, everyone got bikes. Mine was bright red. But I remember lying in bed the night before I got that bike, thinking I'd forgotten to ask Santa Claus for something. Then I remembered: a Baby Alive doll. Those dolls were so cute! I was like, *"Santa Claus, can you please get me a Baby Alive doll? If you're real, please bring me a Baby Alive doll."* The next morning, there it was, neatly wrapped beneath the tree.

Gifts.

It always feels good to receive them.

As a child, I only thought of gifts as toys, but as I got older and started to listen more to my spirit, I found that my family was a gift to me. I also discovered my internal gift: nurturing. Even when I was a kid, I always wanted to be a mother and have a big family. I am thankful for the six children I was blessed with.

Sometimes it's hard, but it's important to recognize and understand your gifts—both the external and internal. If you were given the gift of singing, use it to praise God or to become a pop star.

Whatever you do, make sure you use it wisely. Interestingly, the external gift is not always easy to see. For example, you might not like a certain teacher. Maybe he is too hard on you or you think he gives too much homework (or both). But think about it. All that hard work you put into your homework makes you smarter and more disciplined, and in these regards, your teacher is a *gift*.

So, for me, Christmastime wasn't just about the physical gifts. It was about the birth of Jesus and about family. We'd always have a little function at our house, cooking food that injected the smell of sugary yams and honey-baked ham into the air. And *oooh*, the chitterlings! I don't like them now, but back then, I couldn't get enough of those pigs' guts. My mom taught me how to clean them. And after we'd eat—our bellies fat with yams, ham, macaroni and cheese, chitterlings, pies (we'd bake six of them), and other dishes—we'd sing carols and gospel songs. Then, we'd head to Grandma Lee's or Auntie Barbara's house.

I remember the last time we all got together for a day like this. It's one of my favorite memories because it was the last Christmas before my parents divorced. I was about 10. Looking back, maybe my parents' divorce shouldn't have been a surprise; they argued a lot. But they loved me and I never wanted for anything. Even after the divorce, I had God and my family, so I knew I could get through anything. It would just take some time. A *lot* of time, actually. This had much to do with my low self-esteem. It didn't help that people would always say that I looked like my dad because of my big ole' forehead. I mean, as a kid, what little girl wanted to be told that she looked like a dude? Even if that dude *was* her father.

Nevertheless, I was a tomboy. My friends and I would find abandoned spare tires, grab some boards, and build bike ramps.

Whenever I scraped my knee, I'd rush home, clean up the cut, put a Band-Aid on it and keep it moving. Looking back, I liked that aspect of my personality. I still do. My ability to patch myself up and keep moving. Many kids lose some (or all) of their childhood innocence as they get older and take on more responsibilities. The world isn't always kind. As you'll read in the pages ahead, I've encountered my share of struggles. I've patched myself up more times than I can count–physically and emotionally.

And these days, each patch represents an obstacle I overcame–a victory big or small.

Thankfully, my dad was always there for me. I could talk with him about whatever was on my mind. Sometimes, he didn't even need to say anything; just being around him made me feel protected. When my parents were still married, I'd sneak into their room at night. My dad slept on his side, so I would gently lift his arm up and wrap it around my shoulders then drift off to sleep. Eventually, my dad would tell me to get out and go sleep in my own bed. I'd listen, but the moment my parents fell back asleep, I'd sneak in and wrap his arm around my shoulders.

I think it's important to give fathers their due. The good ones, anyway.

My dad definitely was one of the good ones. I'm the woman I am today largely due to his guidance. My dad wasn't perfect. He made plenty of mistakes, but he could do very little wrong in my eyes. His always being there for me emotionally and psychologically made all the difference in my ability to overcome difficulties in life. Dad and I always looked out for each other. We made each other better human beings.

My mom is another story. I love her, but she and I have never had the same kind of bond. I felt like Mom favored my sisters over me. When I was seven, she forgot me at church. As parents, we make mistakes. The mistake wasn't the issue. I was hurt because when a family member called my mom from the church, asking if she had left anything behind, my mom said, "No, I'm home cooking."

"Well, *Nikki* is here at the church."

"Oh man," Mom said. "Her sister kept bugging me to leave. I must have left without Nikki, accidentally."

In other words, my mom drove all the way home, started dinner, and still didn't realize she was missing me, the baby of the family.

I felt forgettable.

When I walked in the door, my mom said, "I bet you won't fall asleep in church again." I wondered, *"How did this become my fault?"*

That night, my parents argued about the incident. My dad was angry.

I don't think that argument swayed my mother, though, because more than 29 years later, she still refuses to acknowledge she did anything wrong.

When I started having children of my own and took them places, I *always* counted my babies before leaving.

Despite any differences I had with my mom, I did think it was important for children to be raised in a two-parent household. I was devastated when I learned about my parents' divorce. In fact, I was so crushed, I blamed myself. It wouldn't be until later that my dad told me the real reason for the divorce was that my mom was no longer happy in the marriage. This broke my heart and made me resent her a little bit.

Dealing with divorce was tough. It became even more difficult when the judge said I had to live with my mom. I complained about it to my dad, telling him that I didn't think the judge knew what he was talking about—that the judge was terrible. My dad told me the judge felt it was important that girls live with their mom and boys live with their dad. Dad said everything would be okay. I didn't really believe him at the time, but everything *did* turn out okay because eventually, I got to go live with him.

But now he had a new girlfriend, Hannah.

Hannah was great...until she wasn't.

It started at Disney World—of all places. My dad and Hannah took her nieces and nephews and me to *The Happiest Place on Earth*—only for me, it was not so happy because Hannah's nephews kept hitting me for no good reason. They simply lacked maturity. Finally, I decided I'd had enough. When her nine-year-old nephew punched me in the back, I chased him down and pushed him— even though I'd meant to hit him. He wound up falling, skidding across the concrete, face all scratched up. The older nephew, who was 16, punched me in the eye. None of this seemed to concern Hannah. When my dad wasn't looking, she scolded me with a slap to the face.

She added, "Your dad said I could hit you, and you better not tell him." I was confused. My dad didn't hit me, so I knew he wouldn't have given Hannah the okay to do such a thing. Unfortunately for Hannah, she had a camcorder rolling. And the camcorder recorded everything she'd said and done to me. When my dad found out, he didn't speak to her for two weeks.

Eventually, they patched things up. However, Chloe came back into the picture a few years later. Chloe was his former girlfriend he'd known since high school. When my dad went into the service, they'd lost contact, and by the time he was out of the service, she had gotten married. Then, he married my mom, divorced, and hooked up with Hannah. So, at this point, it had been more than a decade. They hung out, though. A lot. In fact, I had a chit-chat with my dad about the situation. He had always respected my opinions; I figured it couldn't hurt to help him figure out who he wanted to be with: Hannah or Chloe.

"*Dad,*" I said, "*what's going on with you and Chloe?*"

"I just got back in touch with an old friend."

"*So, what's going on with you and Hannah?*"

"Whatchu mean?"

"*Well,*" I said, "*how would you feel if someone was dating me or Shareece while dating other people behind our backs?*"

He thought for a moment. "Yeah… yeah…" he said, as the scenario I laid out started to sink in.

The next day, I left to run errands and when I returned, all of Hannah's stuff was gone. I was like, "*Wow! All it took was one conversation.*"

I like to think of life as a series of blessings and struggles—the latter helps me to become a stronger person and appreciate the former. So, my blessing at this stage of my life was family, especially my dad. The special occasions—Christmas and Easter, for example—made me feel more loved and like everything right was with the world.

In upcoming chapters, you'll read about other challenges I have faced throughout my life. Each one has made me stronger in part by forcing me to evaluate my relationships, be they romantic or platonic. I ask myself questions such as: *What am I putting into this relationship? What am I getting out of this relationship? Is this relationship helping me to become a better person? Do I feel I can tell this person anything? If not, why?*

By focusing on both blessings and struggles, we create balance in life. That increases our chances of living our best lives. In other words, we should commit to creating strong relationships and have the courage to walk away from ones of no benefit to us.

If you look at the list below, you will see why I'm still smiling. At the end of every chapter, there is a similar list of questions to prompt you to think and/or write about *your own* experiences, as well as a chart for you to fill out regarding your blessings and struggles. These simple exercises can help clarify where you are in life and where you want to be.

Why I'm Still Smiling...

Blessings
- Loving family
- Special bond with my dad

Struggles
- Insecure about my appearance
- Pushover

How I Plan to Cope with My Struggles
- Insecurity: positive affirmations
- Being a pushover: become more aware of it, then stand my ground

Two weeks before I took my husband Richard to the hospital, my dad had been admitted to a different hospital for knee replacement surgery.

That was *March 12, 2020.*

My son, Kodie, and I and some other close family were visiting him, happy that he was doing well. All of us were hugging on him and joking, but we wanted to be certain that he was better.

"I'm feeling okay," he reassured us. "I'm fine. I'll be up and running in no time."

However, while we were sitting there in my dad's hospital room, Kodie glanced up at me. His eyes that only moments ago were big and bright now seemed worried. "Mom," he said, "I'm not feeling too well."

"Kodie, what's wrong?"

"I don't know. I can't taste or smell anything."

"Ooh," I said, surprised and concerned. *"Well...we're at the hospital. I'll take you downstairs to the ER."*

"No!" Shareece said. "Don't take him downstairs; it's a cesspool of infections."

Aside from my dad's knee surgery, what makes March 12 memorable is the fact that it was also the first day Detroit took action against COVID-19. Robocalls were sent out, telling parents and students that schools would be closed for the next three weeks. This was also the day that people were starting to tear everything off the shelves. After visiting my dad, we went to the grocery store to see if I could buy some things, especially now that Kodie seemed to have fallen ill.

Every.
Single.
Shelf.
Was.
Empty.

So, I would have to make do with whatever supplies I already had. Once home, Kodie immediately walked upstairs to his room to lie down. That's when I really knew something was wrong with him. It was dinnertime and my 12-year-old son didn't want to eat.

Richard said he'd take him to the doctor the next day.

Friday, March 13

At the doctor's office, Kodie was told he likely had a cold or the flu. Though he didn't have asthma, he was given an inhaler and Motrin.

Saturday, March 14

"Babe," Richard said, "I can't taste or smell anything." (Loss of taste and smell still were not yet COVID symptoms.)

Monday, March 16

Richard took Kodie to a follow-up doctor's appointment. When I got to work, I called Richard to check on Kodie. The doctor said Kodie didn't have any COVID symptoms. I was relieved, but looking back on it, I shouldn't have been. I spent the entire day at work interacting with colleagues and clients, not knowing that I could have been spreading a deadly virus. I don't think I got anyone sick. I, on the other hand, had become sicker by the end of the day. I felt weak. After work, I went to Meijer to pick up some over-the-counter medication. Before heading home, I stopped by my dad's house to see how he was feeling. While he wasn't in great condition, there was no indication that he would get sicker.

When I returned home, I had chills surging through my body. I checked my temperature. It was low. After taking a hot shower, I crawled into bed, slinking beneath the covers. At least I wasn't getting any warmer.

Tuesday, March 17

I woke up freezing. It was like I had fallen into Lake Michigan during wintertime. Richard brought me breakfast in bed and when I bit into a slice of bacon, I might as well have been chewing cardboard. I'd lost my sense of taste.

Thursday, March 19

By evening, I had a fever of 104 degrees. Shareece insisted that I go to the hospital if my temperature didn't go down soon. Considering that Shareece also had told me the hospital was more or less a viral cesspool, I was not at all tempted to check myself into the ER. Instead, Richard drove to the store to pick up some Motrin and Tylenol, which brought my temperature down within an hour.

Friday, March 20

My husband woke up to a temperature of 103 degrees. He'd taken a COVID-19 test a couple of days earlier. Pre-existing conditions of asthma and diabetes made him highly susceptible to contracting the virus. We hadn't received the results. At first, we didn't think much of it because his illness hadn't seemed all that strange. But now, I was skeptical. While I wasn't quite sure it was COVID-19, I didn't think it was the flu. The symptoms Richard and I had seemed arbitrary. We'd had the flu before and it never had affected my son, then my husband, then me. We were always able to contain it to just one or two people. But three? No. Something else had to be going on. Later that day, the news reported new COVID-19 symptoms: Loss of taste and smell.

"Great," I thought.

Kodie, fortunately, wound up getting better within a week, but Richard and I were still sick. In fact, we were so sick that our oldest daughter, Amber, had to do all the cooking and cleaning. She was in her senior year of high school.

Richard's taste and smell had been gone for three days.

Mine—two weeks.

JOURNAL

Chapter One

Did you face any challenges with your parents growing up?

What were they and how have they affected you as an adult?

Have you overcome those issues?
Or are you still working through them?

What parts of you are stronger because of it?

Why Are YOU Still Smiling?

Blessings:

Struggles:

How I plan to cope with my struggles:

Chapter Two

The Molestations

ALIYAH. She was an older, annoying family member. Always bullying me. She was bigger, so she did whatever she wanted: took my candy, picked me up and held me upside down, threatening to drop me on my head if I didn't do what she told me. It happened at a family member's house. Even though it was night, it was hot. So hot my bedtime clothes stuck to my sweaty body. There was no AC and sleeping with the windows open didn't do much. I had finally fallen asleep, when Aliyah came in and woke me up. I was agitated.

When I discovered what she was doing—placing me on top of her, then taking off her shirt and whispering something like, "Suck on my breasts"—I crinkled my face and said, "That's nasty!"

She clamped a hand over my mouth. "Shhh! Don't say anything or you'll get a whoopin'."

I was younger than 10. She was nearly twice my age and always beat me up, so I obeyed her. I sucked on her breasts. Then she ordered me to finger her vagina while she made all these sex noises. I was disgusted and clueless and just wanted to go back to sleep. When it was finally over, she got up and left. It was a one-time event, but to this day, whenever she hugs me, I feel disgust rise in my throat like vomit.

Around that same time, another family member started to molest me. Unlike with Aliyah, this was not a one-time event. This was ongoing for two or three years. He'd take me into his basement and touch me where a boy wasn't supposed to touch a girl without her consent. I liked it. I didn't like that he was doing it to me, but the touching itself felt good. These conflicting feelings only made me more confused. Because I was a child, I didn't have the ability to form rational thoughts. This was why I wound up thinking that what was happening to me was normal—or at least *normal-ish*. I knew deep down, though, that something wasn't right because I didn't tell my dad or mom. I told my dad everything, so why didn't I want to tell him about this?

Because I was *ashamed*.

Because I thought what was happening to me was *my fault*.

As the molestations progressed, this family member went from touching me to penetrating me. Surprisingly, it didn't hurt. It felt like... nothing. After he was done, he looked inside my vagina and mumbled, "Good, you're not pregnant." Even at my young age, I was somehow aware that I could not get pregnant, despite barely knowing what "pregnant" meant.

As a society, we have become—or maybe we've always been—Sodom and Gomorrah. I think we can and should do a better job educating our children (and ourselves) about sex in a way they can understand it. For example, we can teach toddlers that no one is allowed to touch the parts of their body covered by underwear unless the doctor needs to take a look down there—and even then, Mommy or Daddy should always be present.

I'm not blaming my parents. In fact, my mom often asked me whether anyone ever touched me. My reply was always the same: "No." My mom was molested, so she wanted to make sure that we never experienced having an unwanted touch, but she never really explained what that meant or how to avoid it. I never told her what happened to me for the same reasons I didn't tell my dad: I was ashamed and blamed myself for getting into that situation. What if my mother blamed me, too? Of course, now I know she would never have done such a thing. But at the time, I had convinced myself that these irrational thoughts were real, and as a result, I grew up having a skewed view of sex. In my opinion, I was robbed of the pure form of what it could be with the right person. Fortunately, therapy later in life helped me a whole lot. In therapy, I learned the most important thing: what happened to me was not my fault.

Unfortunately, many Black people view therapy as taboo—as something that White folks do. This is not the case. You might say your therapy is church. I agree that church can be helpful for some people. Others, however, attend church and gain absolutely nothing because the teachings are going in one ear and out the other. Biblical counseling is another way of tackling issues through the Word of God. It's important to get in contact with a certified biblical counselor. For it to be effective, we must be saved. A certified biblical counselor can also lead us to salvation, but sometimes, the Lord guides us in an unexpected direction.

I encourage people to try therapy—whatever kind of therapy they're comfortable with. The first therapist may or may not be a great fit. Keep trying until you find the right one. If you don't have the time to go in person, you can see a therapist online. Betterhelp.com is a popular site. It is relatively affordable and there is no pressure to sign up. You fill out a questionnaire so they can make the best possible therapist recommendations. If you really feel you do not need to talk to someone, you can try Uplift, an app that tracks your mood and sends reminders to your phone to check in on your progress. Technology makes just about everything convenient. But if you are like me, and need to be in someone's presence, then go in person. The room is cozy. There is a comfortable chair or sofa. It is like what you see in movies, only I was not lying down, making sarcastic quips. It feels good to have someone who is not your family really listen to you. You can see them once a week or however often you decide.

I was nervous at first, but I got over it quickly. My therapist was kind and listened to me intently. Our first session was more of a meet-and-greet. Once I became comfortable, I opened up to her more. She gave me great advice and exercises to do when I had the time, and during the next session, she'd quiz me. It didn't feel like school—it felt like she cared. Do not underestimate the value of having someone listen to you without judgment.

Because of therapy, I was able to become more secure in my identity. In other words, I didn't let what happened to me as a child define me as an adult. While it's important to stay positive, I would also suggest allowing yourself to *be*. If you feel angry, be angry. Feel sad? Be sad. I am not suggesting that you take your anger out on someone. But you should find a space where no one can hear you, then let it all out. That's right, scream. It will feel good. I promise. And after you get it all out, you can sit with yourself. Just sit. I'll bet you will begin to relax.

People make the mistake of thinking they can overcome molestation. I know I did. Molestation is not something you overcome; it is something that you eventually accept has happened to you, including all the pain that accompanies it. Only when you have accepted this can you move on. Moving on does not mean forgetting. You will never forget an experience like that. However, you don't have to let something that has happened to you define you. Always work toward forgiving the person who caused you harm. It's not easy, but it's worth it.

For me, forgiveness came slowly. It did, however, eventually come. Somewhat recently, one of my molesters died and I was asked to sing at the funeral. People may ask how I was able to do it. I'd tell them that I didn't do it for him; I did it for me.

Forgive, but don't forget.

I know "forgive and forget" is a popular phrase, but I think remembering what happened to you is important, if only to minimize the chances of it happening again. In my opinion, God gave you a memory for a purpose. It's how you use that memory that makes the difference.

Once you are born into this world, there is no way to escape it except through death. No matter how difficult life gets, it will end eventually. In the meantime, it is important to not give up, to understand that pain is a part of life.

But so is joy.

I've thought about suicide. Suicide can be tempting, but considering death comes to us anyway, why do it? As a mother, I have eight reasons—my six kids and two foster babies—to keep going daily. We are designed to triumph over tragedy.

But how, exactly, do we do that? Well, it differs for everyone. Still, hearing someone else's coping mechanisms can help you think of your own. Writing down your problems is popular. Call a friend or someone who will listen and comfort you. I like to write songs and sing. You might enjoy journaling. If so, set aside at least five minutes a day and commit yourself to jotting down your thoughts. You'll be surprised how the act of writing can help alleviate your mental and emotional pain. Don't forget to remind yourself of the good things that have happened to you; it's easy to dwell on the negative. Focus on your blessings. Doing so can instill in you *hope*.

Why I'm Still Smiling...

Blessings
- My friends and family
- My church community
- Parents moving out of the neighborhood where my molester lived

Struggles
- Parent's divorce
- Coping with molestation
- Self-esteem

How I Plan to Cope with My Struggles
- Parent's divorce: faith in God and being patient
- Being molested: therapy
- Self-esteem: becoming more aware of when I feel insecure and try to push through it
- Singing/songwriting

JOURNAL

Chapter Two

Did anyone ever take advantage of your youth or naiveté sexually, financially or ethically (i.e., cheating on a test)?
How did it make you feel?

What steps have you taken to understand that it wasn't your fault?

How have you grown stronger in the wake of what happened?

Why Are YOU Still Smiling?

Blessings:

Struggles:

How I plan to cope with my struggles:

Chapter Three

First Love

WE ALWAYS REMEMBER OUR FIRST LOVE. Back in the 10th grade, I wasn't even allowed to date. I could never tell my mom I had a boyfriend. I can hear her now: "Girl, please! *I'm* your boyfriend!"

I remember when I met Braxton. He was always a class clown and a huge flirt, but very sweet. I actually noticed him in ninth grade, but we were just friends. He was that friend who could make me laugh all day. The summer before 10th grade started, Braxton called to tell me his father had passed away. My heart broke for him. Even when we talked the evening of his dad's passing, he was doing what he did best—making me laugh. He wanted everyone to be happy, even if he wasn't. I made banana pudding for the repast for his family.

Shortly after his dad died, our relationship started to change from friendship to boyfriend and girlfriend. If you were a kid in the 80's or 90's, you may remember giving or receiving folded-up, loose-leaf paper with the following question written on it: "Do you like me?" This was followed by two boxes; one marked "yes," the other "no." That's when life was simple. Things were simple with Braxton.

He took me to homecoming, and we had a blast. We were supposed to wear purple, but clearly our mothers did not communicate because I had on purple and he wore burgundy. None of that mattered because all I saw was him. I remember cheesing from ear to ear, thinking this was a real date and we could kiss without sneaking. Both of our mothers were strict, so we could never just go to the movies or dates like that, but Braxton's mom always allowed him to come to church with me on Friday nights for teen ministry. Braxton called me his "monkey." I know it sounds strange, but he said his dad would always call his mom "Monkey." So it was special to me. He even purchased me a black monkey for Valentine's Day, and I kept it for a very long time. He was the only boy my dad allowed at my house while he was not home.

Braxton could have been my first. We made plans to have sex. When you are young and hormonal, you don't always make the smartest choices. I'm glad we never crossed that line. I switched schools and moved in with my dad. Neither one of us can remember when or why we broke up, but we remained friends throughout the years. When we were 14 years old, Braxton introduced me to the man who would later become my husband.

Once I moved in with my dad, I started working at Pizza Hut, where I met Leroy. He was bow-legged. For some reason, I found his bow-leggedness cute. We dated for two years before he asked me to marry him. Mind you, I was 16 and he was 17. At his prom, he got down on one knee and asked me the Big Question. I was awestruck. It was like something out of a movie. When he brought me home, I was floating.

But my clouds came crashing down quickly when, the next day, I told my mom what Leroy had asked me. She was furious. But I was too enamored to care.

My mom was right to be upset. Leroy and I didn't know what we were doing. However, when I had asked my mom about sex, she just looked at me and said, "My mom didn't talk to me about sex and I'm not going to talk to you about sex. Just don't do it!"

This kind of conversation (or lack thereof) is partly to blame for my mom, sisters, and me becoming teen parents. As I said, Leroy and I didn't know what we were doing—we were just following our irrational teenage emotions and hormones. In hindsight, I see how we shouldn't have rushed into things. We were still kids, and while I was faithful, he was sticking his thing into every girl who smiled at him.

I found out the hard way one afternoon, when my friends and I decided to go to his apartment for lunch. Instead of food, a cheating boyfriend was on the menu. On one hand, I was mad at Leroy for cheating. On the other hand, I still desired him. He literally tattooed my name on his arm. To me, that was permanent. That tattoo, to a degree, defined our relationship. When you are 16 or 17, you make impulsive decisions that can affect your entire life.

It was hard to let him go; he was my first positive sexual experience.

This is what girls have to watch out for: having sex with a boy changes things. Girls become attached because they are giving their body to someone else and that means something to them. Sex is an investment in a relationship, whether the relationship is casual or serious. I'd even argue that sex, for girls, is more serious because we are the ones who could end up pregnant. There is also a matter of sexually transmitted diseases. Leroy, as is the case with many boys, saw it differently. He wanted to mess around, which at his age was okay. He simply should have let me know, so I could have decided whether I wanted to stay with a boy who wanted to play the field.

I had always believed in saving myself for marriage. But being a teenager in love sometimes clouds long-held convictions.

Nevertheless, as time went on, I decided to leave him.

Because we were only teenagers at the time, making adult decisions was not our strong suit. Leroy did not know how to be a good boyfriend because he lacked the proper examples. One of the most important things we can teach our teenagers is to love themselves before they attempt to love someone else. When two people are mature enough to be in a relationship, they can grow it into a friendship, and it can be a beautiful thing. A relationship is give and take. It requires trust. Trust is earned. And being in a relationship does not mean you have ownership of that person. They do not belong to you. Trying to monopolize the people we are dating is unhealthy.

Controlling men often display these signs:

- They won't let you go out with your friends.
- They won't let you have any guy friends.
- They always have to know where you are or who you are communicating with.

Anyone else been there?

I've learned through experience that usually when a guy is controlling, it has to do with some sort of insecurity on his part. Giving in only fuels his control. Do not let this happen. If your boyfriend or husband is exhibiting any of these signs, you should talk with him about it immediately, and if you cannot find any middle ground on your own, then I would recommend counseling.

Saying "no" is not easy.

It is hard to move on even when you notice these signs. You might try to rationalize it. You might tell yourself that he will change or, worse, that you can change him. Your job is to be the girlfriend. That's it. Change is up to him. And if he doesn't want to change for you now, he won't change for you later. What would his incentive be? If he got you to be his girlfriend by behaving like a jerk, then in his eyes, there is a high risk of losing you if he changes.

If you do not correct bad behavior at the start of a relationship, there is no reason to think that when you are in the middle of one, bad habits will magically disappear.

But then there's the sex.

Sex is a powerful motivator.

In other words, it can motivate you to make stupid decisions. Here is what experience has taught me: If you're the type of person who once you sleep with a guy, you think of him as your permanent boo, it is probably in your best interest to hold off on sex. You don't necessarily have to wait until you're married unless you want to, but you should wait until you have discovered his intentions. Often, if you are not giving it up to a guy, he will go bother some other female. I also suggest that you look for three red flags or three white ones. Generally, anything that happens three times in a row or over a short period is a pattern. So, if he buys you flowers one day, then smacks you once each day over the next three days, you two probably are not a good match.

The white flags generally are easy to spot because they are what drew you to him in the first place: charming looks, or an engaging or fun personality. It is easy to fall in love or lust with a guy you've just met. The butterflies in your tummy; the euphoria of meeting someone new. This is the way I felt about Leroy. I had a lower sex drive, so I was slower to fall in lust, but I became emotionally attached once I got to know him. But when you believe that you deserve someone who is rarely present, nothing good happens. You spend all your time wondering who he is with, whether he still likes you, what you are doing wrong. That was how it was with Leroy, so I cut him loose.

Even though our romantic relationship deteriorated, we've stayed friends.

So, while saying no is not easy, neither is staying in an unhealthy relationship. At least if you say no and walk away, you increase your chances of finding someone who will treat you the way you should be treated.

So, say "no." See how he reacts. If he throws a fit or becomes violent, you'll know you need to leave. Hopefully, you'll notice the signs before the violence strikes.

Why I'm Still Smiling...

Blessings
- *First love*
- *Pastor helped guide me through rough patch in relationship*

Struggles
- *Letting go of my first love*

How I Plan to Cope with My Struggles
- *Faith*
- *Focus on bettering my personal well-being*

Friday, March 27

A week later, Richard and I felt better. In fact, we felt good enough to start joking around again. It was dinnertime. Meatballs and rice were on the menu. Plus, gravy.

Richard said, "You know I make the best gravy."

"How about we let the kids decide," I said.

"Mom makes the best gravy!" they all shouted.

"Richard," I said, chuckling, *"I taught you how to make gravy. So, if you make the best gravy it's 'cause I taught you."*

"You taught me," he said, dismissing my argument, "but I perfected it."

After dinner we watched Invisible Man in the TV room.

Like *normal*.

JOURNAL

Chapter Three

Describe your first love. How old were you (and your partner)?

Was it a positive or negative experience?

How do you feel that influenced future relationships?

Why Are YOU Still Smiling?

Blessings:

Struggles:

How I plan to cope with my struggles:

Chapter Four

Teen Mom

S TAY AWAY FROM HIM!" That's what my cousin Malcom said when I first laid eyes on Michael. It was at church. He was in the choir, but I didn't like him like that. Besides, at the time, I was still dating Leroy. In fact, when I first saw Michael I was like, *"Oh. He's ugly. I would never talk to him."* I know it sounds bad, but that's what I said to myself—not to his face, of course. I wasn't that mean. My nephews and nieces would say to him, "Mister, you have some chandy on yo' teetf. Mister, you have some chandy on yo' teetf." And he'd be like, "Naw, naw, it ain't candy." He was covering up brown stains on his teeth, which he later got fixed.

At first, I wasn't into Michael.

But my cousin kept insisting that I stay away from him. I guess curiosity kicked in. I was like, *"Why does he want me to stay away from him?"* It made the situation daring and that got me excited. So, I decided to talk to Michael.

Our first date was on a park bench. It was a nice, breezy day and as close to nature as you could get in a city like Detroit. Michael and I talked a lot about everything—childhood, dreams, and random things that pertained to that particular day. I learned that he didn't have a good relationship with his father and realized that, like me, he was insecure. By the time I got home, which was late, I admitted to myself that I really liked Michael. At this point, Leroy and I were done.

My relationship with Michael blossomed. Soon, we planned to sneak off to a hotel and have sex. I was staying at my mom's for the weekend and all I had to do to throw the hound dog off my trail was to tell her that I was spending the night at a friend's house. Easy. I was 18, so it wasn't as if my mom was going to call my friend's parents to double check.

Once inside the hotel room, the butterflies in my tummy escalated. It felt as if I were going to vomit. We sat on the edge of the bed, making small talk. He fiddled with my fingers and stumbled through his words. And I was like, "Uh-huh, uh-huh..." There was a moment I thought nerves would get the best of us, and we would decide that it was better to wait.

But that didn't happen.

Finally, he leaned in and kissed me.

Bliss.

That's how I felt as a million thoughts raced through my mind: "*I like this. But what if we get caught? Is he The One?*"

It didn't take long for all those thoughts to melt away and for me to give myself over to the moment. Sex had that effect—the endorphin rush that kicked in as I stripped naked and got between the sheets with someone I loved (or at least thought I loved). It was like a magical potion; I entered an alternate reality where everything was perfect.

Turns out that magical potion had a short shelf life.

A month later, I discovered that I was pregnant.

I was stunned. He and I had only had sex that one time. But I guess once is all it takes.

Pregnancy can be scary for a woman at any age, but for a teenager whose life is just blooming, it can be scarier—especially for Black girls.

Later in life, I was the executive director of the Detroit Pregnancy Test and Help Center. Although I no longer work there, this type of service is where my heart still is—being able to be a voice for the voiceless. I want these Black girls to know they don't have just one choice. They have three:

- Get an abortion (not a choice I personally recommend, but definitely an option).
- Give their baby up for adoption.
- Raise their child.

I discovered that it was far more productive to simply listen to these girls than to tell them what to do. If I let them speak long enough, eventually they would arrive at a decision, or I would find out enough about their situation to help them come to a decision that was appropriate for them. I always made sure my clients understood their options and knew that no matter what they decided, I would be there to support them.

Post-abortion counseling is a vital part of the abortion process because many of these girls feel like they are awful people, like they are going to Hell. They hate themselves. Hating yourself is a dangerous thing—believe me, I know. So, I tried to calm the girls down. Whenever they spoke like this, I said, "That's not true. God still loves you, no matter what happens. We all have done things that we're not proud of."

Working with these young women was a blessing, and every day I was reminded of my own pregnancy scare.

I was a church girl.

What would the community think about me?

What would my mom think?

Mostly, I worried about my dad's opinion. He'd always had a high opinion of me—not just because I was his baby girl, but because of our tight bond. I didn't want anything to undo that, not even a baby. That's why I decided to tell my mom first. Actually, I tried to convince my sister Shareece to do it. *"Can you tell her?"* I begged my sister. I was at her house in the living room. "You are good at relaying information, especially to Mom."

"No, nu-uh," Shareece said, shaking her head.

"Come on, Shareece," I pleaded. *"Do this one thing for me, and I promise I won't ask for anything else."*

But my sister was defiant. "You have to do this on your own."

And that's what I did.

After church, in the parking lot, I asked my mom if I could talk to her. I asked our pastor to accompany me. I think my mom already knew something was up. Her face tightened, and her dark eyes narrowed.

I got more nervous and pretended to pick lint off my dress.

We sat in her car that smelled of perfume.

I tried to speak, but my mouth refused to form the complete sentence, and my tongue clumsily fumbled these words past my lips: "Mom, I-I-I..."

"You're pregnant, aren't you?" My mother blurted. Had it not been for her violent tone, those four words could easily have sounded like mild excitement.

I lowered my head.

I knew she would be upset.

Anger swelled in her voice. "How could you be so stupid?" she went on. "You are too smart to be so stupid!"

Part of me wanted to retaliate, wanted to say something like, *"You're not perfect, Mom—far from it!"* But I knew better. Besides, I was too ashamed to defend myself. How could I blame my mother for being upset? I had deceived her, disappointed her. At 18, I knew the risks of sex: STDs or babies. In some cases, both. I didn't have the right to retaliate. But it would have been nice if my mother had acted like she cared and told me it would be okay.

Instead, she made me feel worse. She kicked me out of the car and decided not to talk to me for three months.

My dad, on the other hand, listened to me and consoled me. "Well..." he said, his soft, brown eyes troubled. "I guess we better get you some new pregnancy clothes."

Though I was kind of relieved by his response, I could see the disappointment in his eyes and hear it in his tone. However, being the man and father he was, he spared shaming me. He knew I was disappointed in myself.

Michael and I continued to date, and I got to know more about his troubled childhood. His dad once called him a disgrace to the family because Michael had forgotten to take his piano book to his music lesson. He was 12. His father died not too long after that incident, leaving behind a son who thought his dad didn't love him all because he had forgotten a piano book. I don't think his dad meant what he had said; he was just angry. People say mean things when they get angry. I know I did, and Michael certainly did. But once the anger subsides, people have a tendency to regret their words, then try to figure out how to apologize. The thing about apologies is that they are tough to carry out. The offender often is too ashamed to admit any wrongdoing, so he keeps it bottled up, like wine, waiting for the perfect moment to pour out his "I'm sorry."

In life, there is no perfect moment.

I'm sure if Michael's dad had known that, he would have apologized to his 12-year-old son that same day.

Michael had lived with his mother until she kicked him out of the house when he turned 16. Considering that she once threw a glass jar full of coins at his head, his being kicked out was probably for the best. When Michael talked about his mother, he'd often call her the B-word. Given how she treated him, maybe it was somewhat understandable.

Still. That was a red flag I should have noticed. Michael never acknowledged that his mother was still his mother. No matter how he felt about her, stripping her of her title because he thought she didn't deserve it was not his choice to make. His mother had brought him into the world. That alone should have demanded at least a modicum of respect. The fact that he couldn't understand that should have caused me to exit the relationship.

But I stayed.

My low self-esteem did not inspire me to ask myself this one intelligent question: *"If Michael disrespected his own mother, did I really believe he would treat me any differently?"*

Who knows? Perhaps even if I had asked myself that question, I might have conned myself into thinking that I was being absurd. Even teenagers who have high self-esteem tend to make questionable decisions.

So, I stayed with Michael. We had our first child, a daughter, Amber. Four months later, I got pregnant again. I was nervous. I didn't want people to start talking, thinking I was some trashy, unkempt woman.

So, we got married.

And our relationship got worse.

One morning, as I readied Amber for church, Michael barged into the bedroom. "Where are your keys?"

He and I went to different churches. His car was not working, so I had planned on driving him to his church in my car.

"Wait," I told him. *"I have to finish getting ready."*

"Just gimme the keys."

"Then how will I get to church?"

He ignored me, grabbed my keys from the nightstand, then darted out the bedroom. By the time I was able to catch up, he'd made it all the way to the car. I stuck my body into the open window on the driver's side and tried to reclaim my keys.

None of this fazed him.

He put the car in reverse and shot down the driveway, nearly causing the side mirror to smash into my pregnant stomach—it would have, were I not quick enough to put my arm in the way.

I toppled to the ground.

He just looked at me, eyes cold, then drove away.

A neighbor saw the whole thing and called the police. When the police arrived, they asked if I wanted to press charges. *"No,"* I said. I still loved Michael and I didn't want my kids' father going to jail. Looking back, I should have pressed charges. Father or not. Husband or not. No man has a right to abuse someone he supposedly loves. If I had pressed charges that day, maybe Michael would have learned his lesson a lot sooner. But then again, maybe not. That's the thing about hindsight; it cannot exist without the choice already having been made.

Anyway, after the police left, I called Shareece, asking her to pick me up. *"I let Michael use mine,"* I lied. I didn't want Shareece knowing my business. *"But can you drive me to his church, so I can get the keys?"*

She drove me to Michael's church.

Inside, the pastor was preaching. Michael was in the music section, sitting at the piano. He wasn't about to act a fool on that piano of his. I knew that for a fact. If he were Superman, that piano was his kryptonite. He didn't want anyone thinking he was a nut. As the preacher continued giving his sermon, I whispered to one of the ushers, a small woman dressed in the typical black-and-white usher jacket. *"Can you please go get my keys?"*

She smiled. "Yeah, I'll get the keys."

When she reached Michael, she leaned in and, I guess, asked for the keys. As she spoke, his gaze caught mine in the back of the church. He had a neutral facial expression, but I could sense that behind his eyes, rage burned. I don't know what set him off that morning, but it didn't take much those days.

Keys back in my possession, I drove to my church.

Problem solved.

But it wasn't.

Really wasn't.

In church, I went into labor.

My sister drove me to the hospital. Once there, I noticed a golf-ball-sized bruise on my forearm. Earlier, it had been just a small bruise. So, seeing this huge protrusion took me aback. Not surprisingly, it also caught the attention of the nursing staff. "What happened to your arm?" one of them asked.

"I have no idea," I said, acting surprised. *"I just... I don't know. I guess I fell."*

"Are you sure?" They didn't believe me at first and kept pushing the issue. "Is everything okay? Do you feel safe at home?"

"Yes!" I said enthusiastically and in a way that made it sound as though they were crazy for asking such a question. *"Everything's fine."*

Convinced, they turned their attention to my contractions. I had dilated three centimeters, which meant I was almost ready to go into active labor.

The problem?

I was only six months along.

The medical team had to stop my contractions, which was tricky.

They gave me various medications, then put me on bedrest. Even so, I continued to have contractions for the next two months. The doctor finally decided to induce my labor at eight months' pregnant and seven centimeters dilated.

I think having children restores your faith in humanity, which was why I gave Michael another chance. Well, there was that and I still had low self-esteem. My having a baby coupled with low self-esteem allowed me to rationalize staying with Michael.

However, not long after I had given birth, we had another big argument at home. I don't remember what triggered it. I just remember that he took the screws off the front doorknob and as I scurried up the steps, he hurled that knob at me and conked me on the back of the head. I fell, right there on the stairwell.

I couldn't take it.

I finally decided to talk to my pastor about Michael's abusiveness. "Tell him to get out of your house," he said.

I looked at him, wondering if he'd heard what I just said about the doorknob to the back of my head. I thought, *"Maybe you got a little lost along the way. I can't tell him that. Are you expecting me to live through this or... naw?"*

So, I told the pastor this: *"You tell him."*

To his credit, he didn't give me an "I told you so" speech and he could have. After all, he had told me not to marry him. "He's not ready," he said. "And frankly, neither are you. Don't marry him." Obviously, my pastor had been right. But now, I was married with two children.

When our son, Aaron, was still a newborn and Amber was eleven months, I decided to stay with my mom for two weeks. I needed the help because I certainly wasn't getting it from Michael. The whole time I stayed at my mom's, Aaron bawled, which put me in a mood because I couldn't get any sleep. Add the fact that my mom and I didn't really get along and it got to a point where I decided my abusive husband was a better option than my own mother. I turned my two-week stay into one.

As soon as I returned home, Michael and I got into an argument. Once again, I have no recollection of what set him off. But he picked me up and pushed me into the couch as I held Aaron. Michael had me in a fetal position while I screamed for him to get off me. I noticed that the baby stopped crying. *"Oh crap! Get off of me. I don't know if he's still alive."*

He let me go.

I looked at my baby, expecting the worst, but Aaron's silence was not because he had been smothered; it was because he was sleeping.

I realized that when I was pregnant with Aaron, Michael and I fought often, and when Aaron was born, nothing changed. The fussing, oddly enough, comforted Aaron. Without the kind of noise two people make when they argue, it was difficult to get Aaron to go to sleep, which was why he kept bawling at my mother's house.

It wasn't long before Michael started to distance himself from me, from Aaron, from Amber, and from his family. One evening, Michael insisted that I didn't go to his band's live performance. I was hurt because of how much music meant to both of us. Whenever I sang, I felt the burden on my shoulders lighten. Though I didn't consider myself a lead singer, I smiled whenever someone came up to me and told me how much my voice moved them. To me, music was where I found my peace and how I connected with people. For Michael to shun me from his performance, I felt as though he wanted to disconnect from me and his family. That night, not wanting to be alone, the kids and I slept at my mom's house.

The next morning, I got a sitter for the kids and went to work. Michael had gone out of town to perform, so later that day when I returned home, kids in tow, I was surprised to see him standing on the porch, face scrunched with a judgmental expression. "Where have you been?" he snapped. "With your boyfriend?"

"What?" I was dumbfounded. *"No!"* I went on, *"I've got two kids—who wants somebody with two kids?"*

"Then where were you?"

"I was at my mom's house."

He acted like he was about to leave. I shrugged, then took the kids into the house. I hadn't been inside long before I heard a bam!

Michael had rammed his car—the type with the flip lights—into the back of my GMC Jimmy.

He got out of the car and busted through the screen door.

I was on the couch, with a screaming kid under each arm.

He ignored them. His dark eyes focused on me and all I could see was rage, Rage, RAGE! He took a few steps toward me, hocked up a wad of spit then went *thht!* His mucous landed in the middle of my face. Before I could react, he reeled his hand back, bringing it down hard on my left cheek. It felt like a Novocain injection. My face went numb.

Michael got in his car and sped off.

You know how you can be somewhere, and you can hear someone, but you don't hear them? That was me in that moment.

Screaming.

I heard *screaming.*

My *kids* were screaming.

I could only imagine what was going on in their minds. Seeing their father assault their mother had to have been scary and confusing. I was scared and confused. This incident was a wake-up call for me.

I was in a daze for about an hour. I remember picking up the phone and calling my pastor. *"I've gotta get out of here,"* I told him, my voice cracking from the emotional blow I was suffering. *"This is crazy."*

"Is he still there?" the pastor asked firmly, trying to keep me focused.

"No."

"Then call the police."

I called the police.

They came.

And like my pastor, they asked, "Is he still here?"

"No."

As the officer got closer to me, he stopped, then craned his neck to the right. "Did you see your head?"

"What's wrong with my head?"

"You have a bruise."

I knew I had been slapped, but not in the head. Michael slapped me on my cheek, so when I touched the top of my head and felt a lump, I was surprised.

"Are you okay?" the officer asked.

I don't remember what I told the officer; I do remember my pastor arriving just as the police were leaving.

"Pack your stuff up," my pastor told me. "Get your kids' stuff. Go to your mother's house. Where's he playing tonight?"

"Cayenne and Chocolate Bar."

"Okay."

The pastor went to the bar.

Later, I got a call from my cousin Malcom—the person who told me not to date Michael. He said, "Did you know that the pastor came to the bar?"

"Yeah."

"He pulled Michael to the side. I don't know what they said, but Michael's head was all hung low when he left."

"We got into an argument and he got so mad that he rammed his car into mine."

"He what? We were wondering why his lights wouldn't come up—like, 'What's wrong with your car, dude? Why your lights ain't coming up?' He told us you hit his car."

"What?"

"Aw, I'm goin' beat his ass."

Malcom and Michael stopped playing together for a while after that.

As for Michael and me, it was the beginning of the end.

When I returned to my house to get my stuff, I discovered that (encouraged by the advice from my pastor), Michael had already been there and had done the same. Unfortunately, he took some things that didn't belong to him.

He was gone—and he left me to foot the bill.

To keep up with the mortgage, I took in two roommates. I still lost the house because one of the young ladies whom I trusted to deliver the mortgage payment didn't. I had given her cash, which she was to use to get a money order and mail it to the mortgage company. She claimed she had mailed it, but she could never find the receipt. I believe she stole it. Lesson learned: handle important money yourself.

I could have asked my dad for the money, but I didn't want to bother him with my financial problems. Instead, I moved into an apartment downtown and by that time, I had filed for divorce.

But my problems with Michael were far from over.

He stopped seeing our kids and would call me, claiming that he was going to kill himself. I never believed him. Of course, whenever people threaten to kill themselves, it should be taken seriously. But it seemed clear in this case that Michael was just trying to make me feel guilty about divorcing him. It wasn't that he wanted me back; he just didn't like the idea of my not needing him, of my leaving him. And he never missed an opportunity to make my life a hell zone.

One day, I got sick. The kids were staying at Michael's house (a.k.a. his mother's place). I went to work at Things Remembered. The second they saw me they were like, "Oh, no. Don't come in here. Just go home." That's how sick I was. So, I went home, took some medicine, and didn't wake up until hours later. I was feeling a little better by then, but far from well. I called Michael.

"Hello?" he said.

"Oh hey, can the kids just stay over there tonight?"

"What's wrong?"

"I'm sick… I took some medicine."

"What? What kind of mother just leaves their kids?"

"Um… you're their dad. It's not like I'm leaving them with a stranger. I just want them to stay over there for a day just so I can get better."

"Oh no," he said, his voice continuing to rise as he uttered an expletive. "Come get these kids. You know I've gotta work—I've got stuff I gotta do."

Mind you, this was probably the first time he had seen his kids in weeks.

I didn't even bother to put on my street footwear. Instead, I slipped into my house shoes and went to pick up the kids. When I got there, his mother answered the door, Amber at her side, Aaron in one of her arms, and something in her other arm. "Hey, you can take these diapers," she said, talking about the thing in her other arm.

Michael appeared in the background, shouting more expletives. Then he said, "Them diapers is staying here."

"*Okay,*" I said, indifferent to Michael's outburst. "*I've got diapers at home.*"

"No," his mother insisted. "Take these diapers. You need these diapers where the kids gonna be."

"*Julie. It's okay. If he wants to keep these diapers here—I'm not about to fight him over diapers.*" I went to go put my kids in the car.

By the time I got one kid inside, his mother was behind me. "Here," she said. "Take these diapers. This is stupid. There's no sense of them being here."

So, as she put the diapers on the floor of the back seat, I started to buckle up Aaron in his car seat. Suddenly, Michael rushed outside and shoved himself into my backside; I could feel his penis as I continued to buckle up the baby. "Gimme them diapers," he snapped, "or gimme the money for the diapers!"

"*You have to back up,*" I told him, "*so I can give you these diapers because I will be damned if I give you money for anything.*"

I let him have his diapers.

And as he stomped toward the house, his mother came out, shouting, "Why you won't give that girl them diapers?"

"*Julie, it is not a big deal,*" I said. "*Clearly he needs them for somebody else.*"

Suddenly, Michael lunged at me.

Then everything faded to black.

When I woke up, I was in an ambulance.

"Hey, are you alright?" a voice asked.

I blinked a few times until my vision cleared and I saw that it was a police officer who had asked me if I was okay. I nodded.

"Do you recall what happened?"

I shook my head.

"What was the last thing you remember?"

"Him lunging at me."

"Okay. Do you want to press charges?"

I'd later learn what had happened to me that night; the chaos Michael caused brought out all the neighbors on his block. I overheard one of the neighbors say, "He was dragging her up and down the street—even his own momma couldn't get him offa her."

Michael's mother was the one who called the police.

"Yes," I told the officer. *"I want to press charges."*

I was done with him.

Michael went to jail, but was bailed out by his mother. I didn't think that made much sense. Why would you call the cops on your son, then bail him out that same night? I guess it was a mother being a mother. I don't think any mother wants to see her child locked up. Michael wound up having to take anger management classes. These classes might have been partly the reason why, years later, he apologized to me for all the suffering he caused.

In the meantime, however, Michael still had a whole lot of screwing up to do.

I don't think I was ever vindictive. I always wanted Michael to have a good relationship with his kids, which was why I cut off child support twice because both times he was over $10,000 in arrears. Mind you, I didn't have to take away his arrearages, but as I said, I wanted to make it as easy as possible for Michael to see his kids. So, he didn't have to pay a cent. Whenever he'd say, "I can't watch them because I don't have any food over here," I'd go grocery shopping and take groceries to his house.

But still, he managed to complicate the situation. One time, he called my house, then put me on speaker phone. The kids were at his place and they were screaming for whatever reason. I was asking what was going on, but he wouldn't respond to my questions. He just kept yelling at the kids, calling me the B-word.

Who says that in front of little kids—your own children—especially ones who were not old enough to understand what that word meant? He was just crazy.

The Bible tells us that women are to respect and that men are to love. This is because it is easier for women to love—not that men can't love—but loving a man or anyone comes more naturally to a woman. But it is harder for a woman to *respect* a man. A woman can tear a man down with her mouth in a split second and not even realize it. It's because sometimes, we don't know when to stop talking.

There were times when I had to tell myself, *"Okay, Nikki, you need to be quiet."*

I remind my kids that everything you think in your head does not have to come out your mouth. Keep it right there in your spirit. It's not that you're not supposed to say it, but maybe it's not the right time to say it. You should give people time to be ready to receive what they need to know.

I learned that the way to deal with Michael was just to let him get off whatever was on his chest. Listening is a two-way street, however, so if only one person in the relationship is doing it, then the relationship likely won't work. That certainly was the case for Michael and me. Even though we had some good conversations, I should have paid closer attention to the negative ones, as well as his reckless behavior.

Once, he drove down a side street much too fast—it seemed like a hundred miles per hour. I wanted to get out of the car. If he would have spun out, he would have killed us. I was like, *"Stop, you are going to kill us!"*

"We're gonna die together!"

"Noooo!"

But then, my teenage brain kicked in: *"Well, he is so passionate about it. I guess he loves me enough for us to go together."* I look back on it, and I'm like, *"Dummy, no! This dude is psycho!"*

Despite that, I don't regret anything. All those thorns from my marriage with Michael helped me to become the strong, triumphant woman I am today. Love yourself first is advice I give to young ladies and to my own girls. Looking for love from someone else, especially a man, is not going to make you feel better. In fact, it will probably lead to your making poor choices based on emotion rather than logic.

I had to learn how to love *me*.

I allowed my low self-esteem to guide my poor choices for far too long. Fortunately, and I guess somewhat ironically, Richard, a man who later would become my husband, helped me realize this.

Why I'm Still Smiling...

Blessings
- Pregnancy: Amber and Aaron
- Marriage

Struggles
- Telling my parents about my pregnancy
- Coping with an abusive marriage

How I Plan to Cope with My Struggles
- Faith and time
- I divorced Michael

JOURNAL

Chapter Four

Do you have children? How old were you when you had them?

How is your relationship with their dad?

If you could have had your same children at any stage in life,
would you have chosen to have them when you did?

What advice will you give your own children about relationships?

Why Are YOU Still Smiling?

Blessings:

Struggles:

How I plan to cope with my struggles:

Chapter Five

Cancer Scare

I BELIEVE EVERYTHING HAPPENS FOR A REASON, AND THAT PEOPLE COME INTO YOUR LIFE FOR A REASON. The year before Richard came into my life, there was Jacob. He was Bahamian, and I found him very sexy.

"You've got a nice smile," Jacob said, as he sat behind his desk.

I smiled more. *"Thank you. Your smile is pretty good, too—not as nice as mine, but I like it."*

We laughed.

It was supposed to be a job interview, but it turned into a flirt session. When it was over and I was on my way home, the HR department called me. *"Hello?"*

"Ms. Denise?"

"Yes."

"This is Tammy from HR. You must've done an amazing interview because they want to hire you full-time."

"Really? Wow, that's great—thanks!"

Life was going well. I had a handsome man flirting with me *and* a new job.

When I started training, there was another woman in my class who she spoke bitterly as she said, "They offered me a full-time position, but they needed to do a contingency because they had already pulled too many spots."

"*Ooooh, dang!*" I thought. I wondered whether Jacob pulled some strings so that I could get hired. I thought that was messed up, but all I could tell her was this: "*I'm so sorry about that.*"

As I continued to work at my new job, Jacob and I kept flirting until one day, he asked, "Would you like to go out some time?"

I had mixed feelings. I wanted to go out with him, but I had to point something out: "*You're my boss.*"

"So?"

"*Well, what happens if it doesn't work out?*"

"Okay, I respect that."

Two weeks later, one of our coworkers was having a party and invited Jacob and me. Jacob turned to me and asked, "Can I at least pick you up for the party?"

I thought about saying no, but changed my mind, "*You know what, screw it. Let's go.*"

He grinned. "I want to take you to the movies before the party."

"*You think you're slick,*" I said.

We had an amazing evening.

After that first date, our workplace flirting turned into workplace kissing. We'd sneak off somewhere and make out like teenagers even though he was 28 and I was 22. I was happy with the arrangement. It made going to work fun. Anyway, the first time we were intimate, he looked into my eyes and said, "I think I love you."

And I was just like, "*You think? Or you know?*"

He smiled.

We were inseparable after that. Jacob raised the bar for all the other dudes out there. He made me realize what it truly meant to be treated like a woman. He never let me pay for anything—even if it was his birthday. He'd say, simply, "No, I've got it."

He'd have flowers delivered to work. Once, he had a little bear delivered. It was dressed up as a doctor. In fact, it was dressed exactly how he dressed for work: a collared shirt and khakis. He would tell me later that the bear was so I would think of him when he wasn't around. Shortly after, he bought me a diamond necklace. I thought, *This can't get any better."*

And it didn't.

One night, he touched my breast then stopped.

"What is it?" I asked.

"Baby, you have a lump in your breast."

I sucked my teeth. *"No, I don't."*

"Yes, you do. When we go to work tomorrow, let me ultrasound it."

"Fine."

So, the next day, he gave me an ultrasound. "Baby, you have a lump in your breast."

"I'm 22. It's nothing."

"No, you need to go to the doctor. Go get it looked at—it's tiny right now."

A month went by. Jacob asked, "Did you make an appointment?"

"No."

"You better go get that taken care of."

So, I finally made an appointment. The doctor confirmed what Jacob had told me. "Denise," she said. "There's a lump there. Let's at least have it looked at."

She sent me to another facility for a scan. The tech said, "There's a lump, but it's probably nothing. It's definitely not cancer." Those last four words were verbatim.

As a 22-year-old, those four words were all I needed to hear. I was ready to leave. And I did.

That evening, the doctor called, "Denise, I know they think it's nothing, but even though they think it's nothing, let's just take nothing out. Let's just have a surgeon remove it and let us biopsy it." I pushed back a little, because I really didn't want to have surgery, but she finally managed to talk me into it.

It had been weeks since the surgery. At this point, I was working at the National Institute of Technology as the registrar. That morning before work, my pastor called to ask if I'd heard anything from the doctor.

"No," I said. *"No news is good news."*

Later that day, at work, someone from the hospital called. "We need you to come in."

"What? Why?"

"Come in and we'll tell you."

"No, I can't just come in. I've just started working here. I'm in the middle of training, but you can tell me there's nothing wrong over the phone."

"We really need you to come in."

"I really can't. I don't want to make them feel like I have a bunch of issues going on and need to take off work."

"This is important. Don't you think your health is important?"

"Listen. I have two kids to take care of and I don't need to lose a job because I went to a doctor's appointment. You can tell me there's nothing wrong over the phone."

He sighed. "That's just it. I can't tell you that."

"Well, what is it that you need to tell me?"

"I need you to come in here."

"I really can't."

"Okay...the lump that we found was *cancerous*."

I heard him, but I didn't. You know? If this had been a movie, the camera would have zoomed in on my worried face, all sound gone. That day, I discovered that there was something worse than bad news: CANCER. I don't remember exactly what I was thinking, but it was something along the lines of, *"How could this happen to me? I am 22. I am 22. I am 22."* All the times I had repeated it to Jacob, to my doctor, and to myself, at that moment, I could no longer deny the obvious: cancer didn't care what age I was. Even at 22.

"Hello?" the doctor said. "Hello, are you there?"

"No, what did you say?"

"The lump is cancerous."

I got quiet again, then I started crying, *"I'm gonna die!"*

"Can you come into the office now?"

"Yeah, yeah. I'll be at the office."

I scheduled an appointment then hung up.

I went to the bathroom to clean my face, then returned to my computer.

"Are you okay?" the woman who was training me asked. "Before you were engaged, asking questions. Now you're just staring into space."

"Yeah, no. I'm not okay. I just got off the phone with my doctor and

they told me that I have cancer."

"Oh my God!"

Now I was really crying. *"But I just got this job."*

"Screw this job! Are you kidding me? Go home. You need to go home. You're not even in a place to continue paying attention to this."

When I got home, I called my mom then my dad.

"Don't tell Shareece anything," I told them, specifically my mom because she had a big mouth.

I figured I'd go see Shareece. She was in the hospital. Shareece was really going through it because a couple of days ago, she had given birth prematurely and her baby weighed just one pound, four ounces. At the hospital, Shareece and I were just talking, talking, and talking, then my mom came into the room and almost immediately fell to her knees. "You need to get a second opinion," she cried.

I told you she had a big mouth.

When she found out about my diagnosis, Shareece decided to name her daughter after me, Kelsey Denise. Unfortunately, seven months later, her baby girl would succumb to illness that came with being born prematurely. I decided to name my next daughter after myself and Shareece's deceased child: Kelsey Denise.

The following day, I went into the doctor's office. "Denise," he began, "the reason why your results took so long is because you have a very rare form of cancer."

The cancer he was talking about was *dermatofibrosarcoma protuberans*. The fact that it was rare made it scarier because I couldn't even get a survival rate; the medical team was basically winging it. Eventually, the doctor revealed that three different labs ran tests just to figure out the kind of cancer I had.

"Did you have some kind of trauma?" he asked. "Because this cancer generally stems from some type of traumatic event."

Maybe my husband—my ex-husband—punched it into me, but I don't know of any recent traumatic experience.

"Okay. Well, we need to send you back to surgery so we can remove two inches of tissue to make sure the cancer has not spread within your breast."

I took his advice, and to my relief, they said the cancer had not spread. However, to this day, I see an oncologist. At the time, the oncologist did a complete body scan to make sure there was no more cancerous tissue. He discovered another tumor on my ovary. I started to cry. *Why do I keep getting all this stuff?*

I also had to go see a different oncologist because my current doctor did not specialize in my "lady parts," as he put it.

I told my family I needed to see another oncologist, but they did not understand why. They wanted to go to the appointment with me; I told them no. They all listened except for Shareece; she wasn't taking no for an answer. So, she came with me to the hospital. I didn't tell her that it didn't have anything to do with my breasts, but she should have known when she walked into the OB/GYN office. When the doctor told me to drop my pants, Shareece said, "Why you need her to take her pants off to look at her breasts?"

The doctor looked at her, then at me. "Apparently, your family doesn't know why you're here, so are you going to tell them or shall I?"

"You know what, you go ahead."

"Okay," he said, turning to face Shareece. "I need her to take her pants off because we're about to do an ultrasound, and we're going to put the scope in vaginally because she has a six-centimeter tumor on her left ovary."

"What?" Shareece exclaimed. "Why do you get all of this? What is going on with your body?"

"I don't know."

She started crying.

"Shareece, I can't comfort you right now. I need you to get yourself together because you're not helping. This is exactly why I didn't want anybody to come." Eventually, Shareece calmed down.

When they removed the tumor, they also had to remove ninety percent of my left ovary.

I owe Jacob a thank you—more than a thank you, but I don't know any other way to show my gratitude. Were it not for Jacob's handsy behavior, I might not have known I had cancer until it was too late.

Speaking of Jacob, we eventually broke up.

One day, he said, "I'm moving to Ohio and I want you to come with me."

"I can't," I told him.

"Why not?"

"Because I have children. I can't just uproot their lives to go live with you in Ohio."

He was hurt, but he understood. So, our relationship ended. At least on a romantic level. We're still friends, though. After COVID-19 hit, he called to check on me, asking if I needed anything. He was big on health and gave me lots of health recipes, many of which I never really followed up with, but I did appreciate the thought.

Anyway, cancer is no joke.

I did learn a lot about myself, though. I learned that I was stronger than I thought. A lot of that strength came from family, especially my kids. I refused to let anything take me away from them. Cancer was no exception. I also learned that eating healthily and regular exercise both contributed to my having a better understanding of my body. I observed how positively my body responded to a better diet and getting into shape. When I had the tumor, I lost a lot of weight and I lost it really fast. I hadn't thought anything of it because I had already wanted to lose weight. However, I didn't know that losing so many pounds as quickly as I did was not a good thing.

Now that I am dieting and exercising properly, I won't make that mistake again.

My cancer also helped me to manage my time better. Before, my focus was on everyone else. I didn't want people to know that I was ill because I didn't want their pity, which, to me, would have made my whole situation scarier. But if you can, I do recommend turning to your family for support.

By the way, the tumor on my ovary was benign. The doctors think maybe it was a twin that just didn't pass with either Amber or Aaron. They thought this because when they did a biopsy, they found hair and little teeth inside the tumor.

Why I'm Still Smiling...

Blessings
• Family

- *Jacob*
- *All the doctors who kept me informed*

Struggles
- *Cancer*

How I Plan to Cope with My Struggles
- *Stay informed*
- *Surround myself with people who sup-
  ported me but did not feel sorry for me*

Everything was getting back to normal. That's why I was shocked when Richard texted me from our bedroom the next day, unable to breathe. We were both getting better, then I was leaving him at the ER in a wheelchair.

The entire drive home from the hospital, I kept calling him to make sure he was okay. When I got home, I parked in the driveway and just sat there.

And cried.

For an hour.

I couldn't face my kids. I couldn't tell them that everything was going to be all right because at that moment, I didn't believe it. So, I called my best friend, thinking she would calm me down. She was always calm. She could tell you off without raising her voice. "Sis," she said. "Sis, I need you to calm down, and tell me what's wrong."

I was a hot mess. My words, like my emotions, were all over

the place.

"I really want you tell me what's wrong," my friend continued, "but I need for you to take a breath."

I did.

Then I did again.

And again, until I was finally calm enough to say, "*I had to take Richard to the hospital. He couldn't breathe, and then he passed out.*"

"What?" Now she was flipping out, which jerked me right out of my moment of tranquility. Eventually, she got it together, but it was clear she was almost as scared as I was.

When I got off the phone with her, I was still in the car. Richard texted me.

Saturday, March 28, 10:01 p.m.

Richard: *Babe, I'm okay. I'm waiting for them to take me to get an X-ray on my chest. I love you so very much.*

When I got that text from him, a wave of relief came over me. Immediately, I got out of the car. I was barely inside the house before our son Kaleb came running up to me, all teary-eyed. "What's wrong with Daddy?"

I showed him Richard's text.

"Oh, okay." Kaleb scurried back upstairs and returned to his video game. That bit of digital reassurance was all he needed.

Me: *Richard, are you sure you're okay? How is your breathing? I love you more than you know.*
Richard: *A lot better. They have me on oxygen. My*

chest still hurts.
Me: *Are you sure you're okay? I need you to keep your phone on. Please keep me updated.*
Richard: *Yeah, for the most part. I'm burning up. Even though I don't have a fever. My chest hurts. I will definitely keep you updated.*

That was at 10:05 p.m. At 10:21 p.m I texted him again, asking if he was there.

No response.

Sunday, March 29, 6:42 a.m.

Richard*: I am sorry babe. I didn't have my phone on me last night. I had two more episodes where I passed out in front of the doctors this time. He said he is admitting me, but they have no beds available yet, so I am still down here in the ER department.*
Me*: Ask the doctors what they think about you passing out.*
Richard*: My body was fighting a virus, and they're going to send me home, she said. My breathing is a lot better and I feel okay now.*

9:22 a.m.:

They took him off oxygen.

9:46 a.m.:

They put him back on oxygen.

Later he texted me, explaining the situation.

Richard: *It's only on four, though. Last night I had a mask on, and it was on fifteen.*
Me: *Why? You couldn't breathe? Ask them could you be sent home on an oxygen tank since they said you're gonna come home. Are they gonna send you home with it or no?*
Richard: *I don't know. My lungs are weak, I guess. I don't even know. They got me hooked up to a bunch of machines and the machines just started making noises until they turned on the oxygen.*

Richard told me that he was unaware of his inability to breathe; the machines communicated this to the hospital staff.

12:18 p.m.

Richard: *The nurse took some more blood.*

12:32 p.m.

Me: *Did you get the results from the other blood tests? What are they looking for?*

No response.

2:46 p.m.:

Me: *Are you okay?*

No response.

3:34 p.m.:

Richard: *Yeah, Baby. I'm sorry. I was asleep. I think I shit on myself last night a bit.*
Me: *Oh no, did they clean you up? I can bring you clothes.*
Richard: *No. I don't think they know. Hell, I didn't know until I just now repositioned myself and it smells. I took a shower before I got here last night.*
Me: *Ask your crazy nurse can you take a shower.*
Richard: *Yeah, I am, once I get someone down here. They're swamped in this place.*
Me: *Press your nurse button.*
Richard: *I have been a bunch of times.*
Me: *What is the percentage on your phone?*
Richard: *Fifty-three percent.*
Me: *Okay, limit to only contacting me. I'll gather you some underwear and stuff, and bring it up there.*
3:49 p.m. Richard: *Okay, thank you.*

JOURNAL

Chapter Five

Have you ever had a health issue?
What was it and how did you find out about it?

Did you ever wonder "Why me?"

Where did you seek support?

*How can you offer meaningful help to others
who are walking difficult paths?*

Why Are YOU Still Smiling?

Blessings:

Struggles:

How I plan to cope with my struggles:

Chapter Six

My Husband, Richard (Part 1)

I'VE KNOWN MY HUSBAND SINCE I WAS 14 YEARS OLD, BUT WE DIDN'T BECOME CLOSE FRIENDS UNTIL ADULT-HOOD, WHEN HE TOLD ME HE'D HAD A CRUSH ON ME SINCE BRAXTON INTRODUCED US WHEN WE WERE TEENAGERS.

On more than one occasion, I awakened to him staring at me. One time he said, "I can't believe I'm married to you."

"Well, believe it," I told him. *"We have several kids now. This is your life."*

He cancelled a few dates due to work obligations before we finally went out on August 1, 2016. This would turn a lot of women off, but it attracted me to him because it showed how hard-working he was. Finally, we went out to breakfast.

Bob Evans on Middlebelt Road.

I ordered the bacon, ham and cheese omelet, and hash browns with onions on the side. I scarfed my food down before he finished his. "Dang," he said, "You eatin,' eatin'. Can I get you anything else?"

"No, I'm fine," I said, smiling.

"Most girls eat a little bit, tryna' be all cute, but not you. You sure I can't get you anything else?"

"Yeah, I'm good."

My appetite impressed him again on our second date when he ordered the XL platter at Famous Dave's and I asked for the same thing. He actually bragged about this to family and friends, saying, "She was eating what I was eating."

Richard and I were compatible from the start. I didn't mind his canceling dates and he didn't mind my big appetite. Early on in our marriage, Richard told me, "I'm going to treat you the way a man is supposed to treat a woman." Unfortunately, in the beginning—the first four years—that's not how it turned out. Those first years were treacherous.

He was not abusive.

He was the opposite of Michael.

When things got tough, Richard had a habit of leaving.

I was 23 and he was 22. Still relatively young. I had two kids prior to meeting Richard, and I got pregnant soon after Richard and I were married. This was my second marriage, so I had a basic understanding of how it worked. This was his first marriage, and he didn't fully understand how to be a husband. Basically, Richard was naïve. He always wanted to see the best in everybody—a good quality, but one that occasionally had to be reeled in. Somebody told me a long time ago that in order to have a wedding, there needs to be a funeral. In other words, you have to bury some of your single ways to create this new life you want to have.

This was something Richard didn't understand during the early years of our marriage. For example, he would talk to his ex a lot, mostly because he was her son's godfather. Mind you, her son was conceived because she cheated on Richard and got pregnant, then when they broke up, she asked Richard to be the godfather.

None of that bothered me.

I trusted Richard.

But I didn't trust her.

Especially when I discovered that her two-year-old son would stop calling Richard "Daddy" whenever his biological father was around. I thought that was strangely intuitive for a toddler to know. I reasoned that there was no possible way a toddler would know something like that unless he was told by an adult. I knew Richard well enough to know that he wouldn't do that, so it likely was the boy's mother.

So, now she—Richard's ex—had become a problem.

Not only was she trying to get Richard to play Daddy, but she would call or text him at all times of the day and night. To me, that was not a friendly relationship. That was something else. That was something more intimate. As a woman, I suspected she was testing him to see how far he'd go.

People will do what you allow them to do.

When I confronted Richard about it, we had a big argument and he left. I was pregnant with Kodie at the time.

It took another man—one of his friends—to let him know that his relationship with his ex was inappropriate.

After cooling off, Richard came back and said, "Talk to her, so you'll see there's no reason for you to be upset or worried."

"I'm not worried," I said firmly. "But what I'm not gonna do is allow her to come in between our marriage."

He didn't have much to say to that, but at least I had given him something to think about.

Aside from his bothersome ex, another thing that strained our marriage was the habit Richard had of running from his problems.

Whenever there was something that he felt had become too much, Richard would just walk out the door, leaving me to explain to our kids why he was gone. It was easy because Richard worked long hours and often worked out of town, so our kids figured Daddy was simply working.

But the third time he walked out, I told my family that I was done with him. At this point, I was pregnant with Kaleb. Richard tried to come back, but I said, "I'm done, Richard. I can't do this."

He called our pastor. This was a surprise because a few weeks earlier, he had joined our church and I suggested that we talk to the pastor about our marital problems. He frowned at that.

"He always takes your side," he said.

"That's not true," I said. *"If you knew him, then you'd know that he always sides with what is right."*

So, when I told him that I was done, Richard called the pastor who then called me and pleaded with me to let him come home.

"He left," I told the pastor.

"Let him come home," the pastor repeated.

I let Richard come home, but he had to sleep on the couch.

The next day, we talked with our pastor again. But by then, I was mentally exhausted. Everything sounded like Charlie Brown: *whaa-whaa-whaa.* Still, I tried to work things out with Richard. We went to marriage counseling and over time, he did a complete 180. He helped around the house and stopped running away from our problems. He even stopped communicating with his ex so often. We both were learning that marriage was about listening and not necessarily responding. In other words, we had to learn to take criticism.

During counseling, we made a list of pros and cons about our marriage. This was useful because it helped us see our flaws. Richard felt like he had more flaws than me, which I didn't think was true. Nonetheless, the source of many of his flaws could be traced back to his childhood when he saw his mother placed into a mental institution. Richard felt his father was more concerned with his new stepmom in Canada than with his duties of father-hood. Richard had to become the man of the house, which meant he had to take care of his siblings. I was amazed at how he could grow up in such a negative environment and be so loving.

It took about a year to work out our biggest marital problems and a few more to work out smaller issues. By year five, we had an amazing marriage. Richard was always good to me and our kids, and he treated Amber and Aaron as his own.

But other challenges were on the horizon.

Why I'm Still Smiling...

Blessings
- Marrying Richard

Struggles
- Marital problems

How I Plan to Cope with My Struggles
- Counseling
- Faith
- Patience

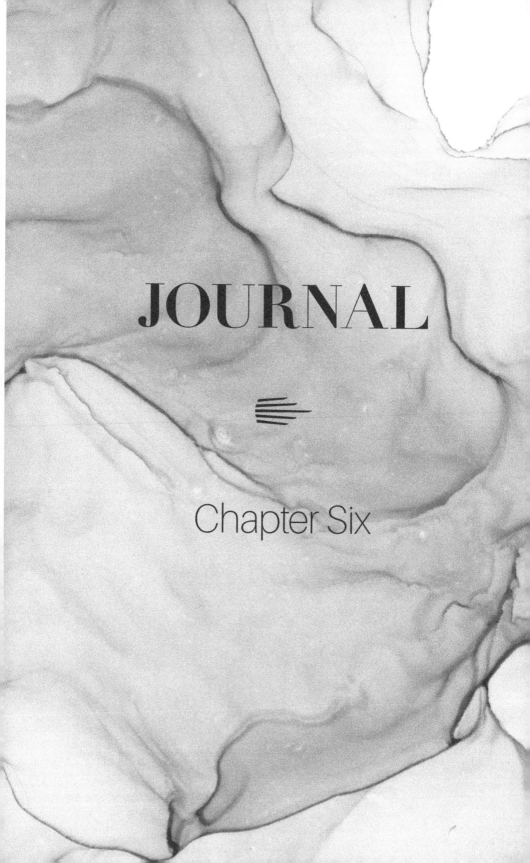

JOURNAL

Chapter Six

Do you think any relationship can be perfect right from the start or do two people always need to work out differences first?

What things have you learned are the
most important traits to look for in a partner?

Do you think it's more important to know what you want
*or what you **don't** want?*

Why Are YOU Still Smiling?

Blessings:

Struggles:

How I plan to cope with my struggles:

Chapter Seven

My Husband, Richard (Part 2)

O N NOVEMBER 29, A MONTH AFTER OUR WEDDING, I VISITED THE DOCTOR FOR MY ANNUAL CHECKUP. He asked, "When was the first day of your last period?"

"Oh, I can't forget that! It was my wedding night—October 29th."

"It's November 29th."

"I know."

"You're late."

"Am I?"

"I can give you a pregnancy test."

"No, no. I can take one at home." I don't know why I didn't want to take it there.

I picked up like 20 pregnancy tests, put them all in a giant cup and peed on them. Then, I spread them out on a paper towel and looked at the results: they all lit up.

"Oh my," I said to myself. *"I am about to have a baby."*

I texted my husband at work: *"Can you pick me up for lunch?"*

At this point, we were still newlyweds, so we were still in the honeymoon phase of our relationship; impromptu lunches were our thing.

He came and picked me up for lunch, and as he drove down

the street, I said, *"I got fired from work."*

"You got fired? Oh, that's terrible, but it's gonna be okay. I make enough money."

I handed him a wrapped-up note. *"Look at this pink slip they gave me."*

"What?" He looked at the note. "This is not even pink." As he drove, he struggled to open it. "Wow, they really folded this up."

I couldn't take the anticipation anymore, so I said, *"It says, 'I'm pregnant.'"*

Almost immediately he started zigzagging.

"Please, just drive," I said. *"I didn't know you were gonna kill us."*

"Oh my God!" He was so excited.

One of my favorite moments ever.

Nine months later, Kodie was born.

Easy pregnancy. Quick delivery. Perfect baby. Richard was in awe.

Seven months later, I was pregnant again. This time, I miscarried.

Miscarriage. One of the worst things a mother can suffer: losing a child before even getting to know him or her. When all your hopes and dreams are literally inside of you, but they never come to fruition, you are left wondering what could have been. That name, now unused. How would she (or he) have lived up to this name? I questioned God more thoroughly because it didn't make sense for Him to take a baby before the child had a real chance at life.

It depressed me.

It angered me.

And I was mad at Richard because he didn't really understand what I was going through.

Prior to my miscarriages, things were going relatively well, except for some minor hiccups.

"Don't worry," he said. "We can have some more kids."

*"But what about **that** kid?"* It frustrated me that he didn't understand my feelings.

Three months later, Richard and I decided that it was best if I had my tubes tied. I was afraid of miscarrying again. The very thought of having to tell someone else I was pregnant and then not pregnant was too much for me. Wondering what I did to lose my baby. Getting a tubal ligation to prevent the pain of miscarriage was my only option. A doctor ran a blood test, making sure I wasn't pregnant and the results came back negative. Twelve days later, my dad took me to the hospital because my husband had to work. They placed a surgical cap on my head and gave me a gown and footies. As the nurse wheeled me to the surgery room, she said, "Wait, we have to do a urine test."

"No," I said. *"They already did that."*

"I could get fired if I don't do it."

They wheeled me into a makeshift room that was only a "room" because a curtain separated me from the outside world. It took a long time to do the urine test. I had been sitting in the room for 25 minutes. They were just behind the curtain. I could see their feet as the nurses argued about something. One of them poked her head from behind the curtain and said, "You can't have this today." The concern in her voice made it sound like something was wrong with someone else.

"Oh my God," I said. *"Is my dad okay?"*

"Your dad?" She was confused.

"Yeah, he's in the waiting room. Is he okay?"

"Yes, I think so."

"Well, why can't I have it?"

She hesitated a few seconds before she said, "You're pregnant."

Now I was confused. Pregnant? Impossible. *"No, I'm not,"* I snapped. *"You dipped somebody else's urine. Do you need me to drop again so you can test it right because you obviously did it wrong?"*

"No... did you put the cup on the sink and—"

"Yes. I did."

"Well, you're pregnant."

"No, I'm not. Go get me a doctor. Because you don't know what you're talking about. Go get me my doctor because who gets pregnant in 12 days?"

"Apparently you." She got my doctor.

When he came into the room he said, "Congratulations, Mrs. Chandler."

"No. No. No. I did not just get pregnant. You just took my blood. That's the most accurate test you can take."

"Yeah, it's a miracle."

"No, no, I'm not leaving here until y'all take my blood again. I need to see from a blood test, not a pee test. I need you to take some blood."

"Okay, we'll take your blood again just to be sure."

While I waited, my dad came in and I told him what happened. He said, "That don't make no sense. You came here to get your tubes tied and you left with a baby."

An hour later: "You are pregnant," my doctor said.

I was shocked. Richard was thrilled.

Two months later, I miscarried.

I was like, *"God, what did I do? Because I tried to get my tubes tied to stop this from happening. Why did You get me pregnant just to take my baby?"*

I went through the whole thing again: the sadness, the depression, the anger, the lying around. The only thing different was that Richard had a better understanding of how I felt, and I think he could feel it, too—my pain.

"Let's go on vacation," he suggested.

"Okay."

We went to Wisconsin Dells for the weekend. It was a nice, brief getaway that helped us to relax, connect, and slowly accept what had happened to me, to us.

Two months later, while I was in class (finishing up my bachelor's degree), I started to feel really sick. I left school and took a pregnancy test. I was pregnant again. By now, I had been pregnant three times in one year. This time, I didn't tell my husband or anybody else. I didn't feel like getting my hopes up only to miscarry. I was a medical assistant, so I called in my prenatal vitamins prescription. I didn't need to go to the doctor immediately.

However, after my first trimester, I decided to pay my doctor a visit. When I finally told Richard, he was upset, but he said he understood why I had taken so long.

After Kaleb was born, my husband told me, "Okay, we have four kids. We're good. We have a great little setup here."

When he said this, I had an epiphany. I said, *"Yeah, I had four kids vaginally. I'm not getting my tubes tied. You get a vasectomy."*

Seven months after his vasectomy, I got sick in school again. My teacher took one look at me and said, "Ooh, Denise, are you pregnant?"

"Absolutely not. My husband had a vasectomy."

But then I thought, *"Could I be pregnant?"*

So, I went to the supermarket and bought a pregnancy test. They had bathrooms outside the entry doors; I went into one of the bathrooms, took a test, and discovered that I was, in fact, pregnant. I called my husband, bawling. "What's wrong—are you okay?" he asked.

"No, I'm pregnant."

"Oh. Okay, well I hope it's a girl."

"What? Did you hear what I just said?"

"My boy told me sometimes the vasectomies don't work until after a year after you have the procedure."

"That would have been some great, need-to-know information."

Actually, I was glad that his attitude was upbeat; it made me feel better.

"I hope it's a girl," he repeated.

"Me, too."

Kelsey was born.

A year later, along came Mackenzie.

That made two pregnancies that occurred after Richard's so-called "vasectomy." It was clear that my husband had to have another vasectomy. It was also clear that somebody was getting sued. However, when we tried to sue the doctor who performed his initial vasectomy, we learned not only that he had died, but that if we wanted to sue his estate, we would have to give up Kelsey and Mackenzie, as that was the only legal way we could file a complaint.

I guess God decided, in His own mysterious way, to give me back the kids he'd taken during my miscarriages. Kelsey and Mackenzie are miracle babies—conceived despite my husband's vasectomy and my one ovary.

Why I'm Still Smiling...

Blessings
- Miracle babies
- My husband

Struggles
- Miscarriages: I struggled with my faith, wondering why God would do something like this to me

How I Plan to Cope with My Struggles
- Faith: even though I felt God had abandoned me, I also felt He was the only one who could comfort me
- Richard: when he finally began to understand me, Richard was my rock.

JOURNAL

Chapter Seven

Has life ever taken an unexpected turn?

Do you believe in miracles? Fate?

*Have you ever been disappointed only to later find it was the best thing you **never** could have imagined?*

Why Are YOU Still Smiling?

Blessings:

Struggles:

How I plan to cope with my struggles:

Chapter Eight

No Right Way to Say Goodbye

My pastor told everyone about Richard's passing because I couldn't — I didn't want to. Already emotionally exhausted, having to tell everyone that my husband was dead,
I felt, would've killed me, too. I decided that the best place to tell
everyone — mostly, my kids — was at our house. Some close family
members came over, and we all gathered in the front yard, making
sure we were social distancing. Clearing his throat softly, Pastor
May delivered the news about Richard. "We all put our trust in God
to help us get through this, but unfortunately he has passed on."

My kids lost it.

Wails …

And tears.

"Daddy, no!" they screamed. "Daddy, Daddy, Daddy!" I could
do nothing except console them with hugs. I, by the way, was the
only one hugging my children because I didn't want to risk my
kids and other family members getting sick.

Amber started to hyperventilate before she stormed into the
house. I wanted to chase her, but my family all agreed that, for
the moment, I should leave her be.

Then there was Kodie …

My son did something that I just wasn't prepared for. "Okay, Mom," he said, wiping the tears from his pudgy cheeks. "Let's pray."

He was 12.

"Mommy can't pray right now," I told him gently, "but if you would pray, that would be so helpful."

He nodded, then said, "Okay, come on everybody. Hold hands, hold hands. Dad would want us to be strong. Hold hands, hold hands."

Kodie prayed a prayer that dug into my spirit: "God, I ask that you bless my family right now. Give us strength to be strong for one another. Comfort my dad because I know he misses us right now and we miss him. Help my mom to be strong for us and help us to stick together because we're all we have."

My kids slept in my room for six weeks. Amber, an additional two. But maybe sleep was the wrong word; none of us could get any real shut-eye. The weight of Richard's death pressed down hard on our hearts. My focus was on trying to help my kids through their pain, to let them know that we were in this together. No one was alone. If they wanted to talk, we talked. If they wanted to be left alone, I left them alone. It was a fine balance. One of my children talked about suicide. Fortunately, allowing her to talk about it caused the idea to subside. But I am always alert, looking for verbal or physical reassurance that her suicidal thoughts have not returned.

Aside from family, the people in our community were a lifeline. They sent us so many meals and groceries that I couldn't fit them all into my two refrigerators and three freezers. I started to give some of it away to our neighbors and family. My kids and I weren't hungry, anyway. It seemed Richard took with him all of our appetites.

Then came the second blow.

It was on a Wednesday.

Shareece called to tell me that our Daddy wasn't doing well.

The next morning at 5:30 a.m., Shareece sent a family group text: They had to intubate him.

I got a sinking feeling that there would be no positive outcome. When Richard had been intubated, thirty minutes later, he died.

I got out the bed.

I had to tell the kids.

I didn't want another bomb dropped on their world. Losing their father unexpectedly was devastating. Losing their grandfather would be equally crushing, if not more so, because they were already trying to cope with Richard's absence. I woke my kids up and explained to them that their grandfather was in the hospital and that it wasn't looking good. "I just want you to be prepared for anything that could happen." They all seemed to understand, but maybe they really didn't. I certainly didn't.

Why would God do this to me—to us? Again?

Meanwhile, we still had to go to Richard's funeral.

I never imagined having to stand in front of my own husband's casket and sing at his service. I remember walking into the funeral home. It was the first time we had seen him since I dropped him off at the hospital. I was terrified to walk inside. The kids were scared and hurting, as well. To see him lying there, lifeless, was truly surreal. I had to be brave for my children so we could get through this service. I don't like calling it a service because it was anything but. Due to COVID-19 restrictions, the only people in attendance were my mom, my children, me, and Richard's aunt. My kids surrounded Richard's casket as I sang to him. He lay there as if in a deep sleep, listening to my voice. He always thought I had the most amazing voice.

We looked at his casket for about an hour. When I felt it was time for him to be lowered, I collected his little blankets and folded them. Traditionally, this was done by the funeral home, but I wanted to do it. I needed to do it. It was the last thing I could do for him, like tucking him into bed, but instead of saying goodnight, I said goodbye. These small gestures brought me some semblance of closure.

We had a private repast at home. My kids and I were eating at the table, when we heard a buzzing sound. I traced the noise to the buffet. In my throat, a lump refused to budge. There, on the buffet, was Richard's cell phone. His alarm had gone off. It was a reminder: *Pray with Nikki and the kids.*

At this point, we all freaked out. His phone had never gone off with that kind of reminder. I felt it was a direct message from him, so I said, "Let's pray."

This was the beginning of our new journey, navigating life without their dad and without my husband.

My dad was still in the hospital. He had been diagnosed with COVID-19 and placed on a ventilator. We couldn't see him or talk with him, but the nurses called me every day with updates. "Hi, Ms. Chandler?"

"It is."

It was the doctor looking after my father. My heart fell to my feet. From my experience, when a doctor called, it meant someone I loved had died.

"I'm just calling to give you an update. Your dad had you on here as his emergency contact."

"I bet he did. But let me help you. Let me give you my sister's number because I can't do this. I know my dad has me down and if you can't reach her, you can call me. But please. I just lost my husband. I cannot take any more news, whether it be good or bad, over the phone when it comes to my dad's prognosis. Please, just call her and maybe she can text me."

The doctor agreed.

Later, I prayed. I asked God aloud, *"Please do not let my dad pass away on my daughter's birthday."*

Amber's birthday is April 14.

My dad passed on April 16.

God did answer that prayer.

Two weeks later after my husband's funeral, I was back in the same funeral home, picking up my dad's cell phone, shoes, and wedding ring. The only upside to my dad's funeral was that, unlike Richard's, we had a viewing and a funeral service. Also, 10 people were there—still only a handful—but more than what my husband had gotten. My father was a veteran, but because of COVID-19, he couldn't receive a proper military send-off. Fortunately, my son Aaron had completed basic training, so he was able to give my father some semblance of a military funeral. The song "Taps" was played toward the end of the ceremony.

Why I'm Still Smiling...

Blessings
- COVID-19 did not claim the lives of my children or me, which would have left my kids orphans
- My husband's and Dad's funerals gave me closure
- Family, friends and strangers reached out with prayer and food

Struggles
- Being a single parent
- Loneliness
- Trying to stay strong for my children

How I Plan to Cope with My Struggles
- Find support from family and friends
- Therapy, prayer and journaling

- Keep my faith in God
- Have some Mommy Time Out

JOURNAL

Chapter Eight

Sometimes bad things happen to good people.
Have you ever had someone you love suffer or die too young?

How did you handle it?

Did it make you question your beliefs?

Looking back, did you learn anything from it?

Why Are YOU Still Smiling?

Blessings:

Struggles:

How I plan to cope with my struggles:

Chapter Nine

Reflection

Despite all I have been through, my faith has never wavered. Faith is important, especially during a crisis. Even if it's just a little bit, hold onto it. Put it in your pocket, purse, or just grip it inside your palm like a stress ball. Whatever you do, don't let it go. Since the loss of my father and my husband, and ever since an article about my experience with COVID-19 was published in the Detroit Free Press, many women have reached out to me.

I spoke to one woman on the phone for three hours. When her husband died, she didn't have anyone in her house to keep her company. Even though she had family, she told me her family didn't understand how she felt. When I suggested that she felt isolated, she almost immediately said, "Yes, that's how I feel. I feel isolated." I told her she didn't have to navigate this life alone. We check in on each other at least once a month. Other women have shared similar stories, so I decided to start an organization devoted to helping these women who lost their husbands to COVID-19 see themselves through difficult times: Surviving Wives Adopting New Normal (SWAN2). I'm still in the beginning phases of creating the organization I envision, so it hasn't officially launched yet. But I figured I should start with what I have and help who I can right now. My goal is to create a safe space for women to vent, to lay all their emotions on the table (if they choose) without fear of judgment. I advocate strongly for better communication and I believe one of the best ways to achieve this is to let people be themselves, which helps with the grieving process.

So far, there hasn't been a single woman in the group whom I have not seen myself in. A common bond we share is that we all wish that our loved ones did not have to suffer alone—in isolation, like something unwanted. This is one of the worst aspects of COVID-19: to know that someone you love is holed up in a hospital room, sick, possibly dying, and the closest thing to human contact is a text, a phone call, or video chat. Even now, I think about Richard collapsing on that cold, linoleum ER floor. He was all by himself.

By himself.

That bothers me.

Yes, we texted, but I wish I had been there at his bedside when he defecated on himself. I could have alerted the nurses. When he fell, maybe I could have caught him. But mostly, I regret not touching him one last time, holding his hand, telling him that everything was going to be okay. I wish I had been able to look into his eyes and say, *"I love you."*

Also, it doesn't help that I believe had I taken Richard to a superior hospital instead of the one I rushed him to on that pivotal day, he would still be with us. I believe that hospital failed my husband when they didn't take immediate, critical steps that may have increased the odds of his surviving COVID-19. Richard had come in with chest pain and difficulty breathing. These two symptoms warranted a CAT scan. They didn't give him one. They should have given him a D-dimer test to determine whether he had a blood clot, which he clearly did. Next, Richard should have been put on medication—Heparin to be exact; it likely would have prevented the clot from getting bigger.

Had they taken these three simple steps as soon as he arrived in the ER, I believe I could be fussing with my husband right now instead of wearing this urn necklace with his ashes in it.

But I digress.

Although the single mom life is challenging, I manage it. I try to exercise and eat properly. People think exercise needs to be a thousand push-ups a day, then running 30 miles. Yeah... no. Not for me. One of the perks of motherhood is that my kids will always keep me on my toes. But I also walk when I can. You would be surprised how walking 20 to 30 minutes a day can keep your blood pressure in check. Eating the right food is also a must. I strive to eat fruits and veggies. It's not always easy doing these things when you have children, so sometimes I find myself at the McDonald's drive thru. That's ok. The next day, I eat better. Sleep is a priority, too. I have learned that without it, I cannot function properly. Drinking sea moss tea (warning, it is a bit bitter) before bedtime helps me fall asleep faster.

I also practice MTO: Mommy Time Out—my version of mindfulness. It's when I tell my kids not to bother me unless it is an emergency. I go to my room, which is full of positive affirmation quotes and scented candles, and I let myself just...be.

After losing my husband and my father, I took the rest of 2020 off to focus most of my time and energy on my children. I returned to work in February 2021. The challenges of simultaneously working full-time, being a single mom, and navigating the children's schedules have been the greatest challenges of all time. I have worked hard at trying to not drown myself in my sorrow and instead, choosing to press on each day. Some days can be harder than others. There is not a day that passes that I don't shed a tear. I just do it in my bathroom away from my children.

Writing down my thoughts is extremely helpful. I write my husband letters frequently. Whenever I feel like I can't express myself verbally, writing comes in handy. I did this when he was alive, too. When people speak to each other, especially when they are angry, they tend to listen to respond rather than to listen to understand. When a person reads a letter, they usually need to read it two or more times to fully understand what the letter is saying.

Grief counseling has helped me, too. It is good to have someone listen to what you have to say, or even to simply sit with you as you cry or shout.

These are just a few strategies I use. However, sometimes—and I am sure most parents can relate to this—I find myself making it up as I go along.

My kids, like me, have urn necklaces. At some point, I plan to rent a cabin in Gatlinburg, Tennessee. There's a lake where I'd like to scatter some of Richard's ashes. Before his death, we were all planning to take a trip there.

I am trying to make this grieving process as smooth as possible, but it is difficult. Some moments are tougher than others. Holidays, for instance. Christmas 2020 was the first spent without Richard. I pulled out a book called "How it Feels When a Parent Dies." The book has several stories from different children who talk about their feelings. The kids and I discussed the book for two hours. It helped them to put their feelings and thoughts into perspective. And, boy, did they have some interesting perspectives.

Kaleb said, "Mom, anybody wants to date you, they have to talk to me and Kodie. Period."

"Well, Kaleb," I said, *"how do you feel about me dating again?"*

"I don't know how I feel about it. I have to have a conversation with him first, then I can tell you how I feel about him."

Remember, he's 11.

"Mom, yes," Mackenzie said, "I want you to marry again because I want a dad."

"Mackenzie, no one can replace your dad."

This was how most of our conversations about their dad went.

They just have so many different emotions. I was consumed with trying to make that first holiday season since their father's death as special as possible. The three littlest ones, for example, wanted costumes for Halloween. I was never big on Halloween in the past. I only took the kids trick-or-treating one time in their entire lives. I would have done it in 2020, but the pandemic kept us inside. I ended up buying them lots of candy and created a scare zone in our backyard. I made sure the holiday season was memorable, not only because Richard and my dad were not with us, but because I want the kids to believe in all the possibilities the future holds.

And the unexpected happened.

What I couldn't even perceive as being in the realm of possibility turned into one of my greatest blessings. But I've learned over time that when you're faced with unexpected detours, detours still get you to your destination. I remember having conversations with both of my sisters, telling them that my "package" (of expectations for a mate) was so big that I was prepared to be alone and raise my children. Anyone entering a relationship with me would need to not only love, accept, and respect me, but had to do the same with my children. It was hard to believe that a person like that existed somewhere in the world.

Remember Braxton? The one who introduced me to Richard many years ago?

We didn't talk much after my husband and my father passed. As a matter-of-fact, it wasn't until several months afterwards that he texted to check in and we eventually decided to meet up for dinner. We shut the restaurant down. Then, we sat in the car and talked for hours following dinner. Literally hours. It was well after midnight before I decided to go home.

We planned to hang out a few days later. And part of that plan was to watch movies at his house. However, we talked for about three hours before the movie started, so when we finally hit "play," I fell asleep almost instantly. When I woke up, it was 3 am. I rushed home, as I figured my children were worried about me and my whereabouts. They never called once, but at this point, I hadn't left my children alone since Richard's death.

Braxton became a really great friend. We talked almost daily. He kept me laughing. Over time, I realized I had feelings for him. A man who truly understood my "package," genuinely loved my children, and would pray with and for me. What a blessing. I never believed I would have the ability to love again. Braxton has four girls and I have six children and two foster babies. Bridging our blended family has been an amazing adventure filled with laughter, tears, arguing, conversations, and most of all, love.

Most recently, I was diagnosed with a rare kidney disorder. When I talked to Braxton about my diagnosis, he simply said, "Okay. We're riding this together."

I know this new battle isn't too much for God. Just like every other challenge, I will get through this.

I've been through a lot and so have my children. I have only shared a fraction of what we have overcome. It wasn't easy. In fact, it never seemed easy. It was the strength of God, the love and support of my sister, my best friend, my kids, and my will that provided me with the fuel to keep moving forward. It would've been so easy to give up in the midst of adversity. Many wouldn't even have blamed me if I had chosen to. But I couldn't.

I choose to keep walking.

I choose to keep believing.

And as long as there is breath flowing through my body, I will do my best to let my kids know that there is *always* a reason to keep smiling.

JOURNAL

Chapter Nine

What does "faith" mean to you?

Has your faith ever wavered or have you been able
to hold it close through the peaks and valleys in life?

What are your strengths?

How could you use those strengths to help others?

What was the most traumatic event you've experienced in your lifetime?

How has that event shaped your outlook on the world?
Has it made you more negative or positive?
Give examples.

What have you learned about yourself after having read this book?

Why Are YOU Still Smiling?

Blessings:

Struggles:

How I plan to cope with my struggles:

About the Author

 Denise Nicole Chandler is a force to be reckoned with. Not only is she a business owner and widowed mother of six, but she's also made a lasting impact on low-income students when she served as their teacher in the charter school education system. She earned the Transition to Success Award from Matrix Human Services, in which she delivered a heartfelt speech in front of hundreds, and later became the Executive Director of Detroit Pregnancy Test and Help Center. Since the global pandemic, she has been passionate about helping women and children see themselves through difficult times. Denise received her master's degree in Education with a specialty in Family and Community Services from Ashford University. She currently serves as an ELA teacher at Chandler Park Academy Middle School in Harper Woods, Michigan.

Email: DChandler1221@yahoo.com

Printed in the USA
CPSIA information can be obtained
at www.ICGtesting.com
LVHW052310211123
764224LV00012B/556